ON MY PERIOD

On My Period

Poems
by
ELENA PETROVSKA

Adelaide Books
New York / Lisbon
2019

ON MY PERIOD
Poems
By Elena Petrovska

Copyright © by Elena Petrovska
Cover design © 2019 Erin Lee Carman

Published by Adelaide Books, New York / Lisbon
adelaidebooks.org

Editor-in-Chief
Stevan V. Nikolic

All rights reserved. No part of this book may be reproduced in any manner whatsoever without written permission from the author except in the case of brief quotations embodied in critical articles and reviews.

For any information, please address Adelaide Books
at info@adelaidebooks.org
or write to:
Adelaide Books
244 Fifth Ave. Suite D27
New York, NY, 10001

ISBN-10: 1-949180-85-9
ISBN-13: 978-1-949180-85-5

Printed in the United States of America

*To all those who've inspired me, supported me,
and loved me- even while on my period.
To all the periods in the world; no book would be
complete without one.*

1)

I decided to write a collection of poems,
While on my period.
All these poems were written by me
While on my period.
So there are no chapters
Or an organized fashion
Of writing these.
They're pure
And raw
And messy
And this is how they happened
To flow out of me-
Literally.
I hope they're not nasty
Or gross
Or too emotional for you.
I often find
That I'm most sincere when on my period.
The most honest.
There's more spilling out from me than just blood.
Well,
Even my words are bloody
Because they symbolize pain
And suffering.
I just wanted to let
My creative juices flow,
In one way or another.
All I am

Elena Petrovska

Is a woman
Who didn't have a baby this month.
And yet, I'm losing bits and pieces of myself.
Not just this week,
But all month.
I'm losing myself when people don't hear me,
When they disrespect me,
When they don't understand me
Or feel me.
So, if you don't like it,
Blame it on the blood I shed.
You've caught me red handed-
Blame it on my period, again.

2)

Boys who don't get a girl
Find a way to make the whole world swirl.
They blow up schools and malls
Just because they didn't get their pretty little dolls.
They kill and they murder
Because she wouldn't let them get any further.
They think the world owes them a life or two
Because they got emasculated by a few.
These boys-
These boys have a lot to learn.
They end up shooting bullets
Because they're not shooting sperm.

3)

Our girls,
Our girls are slipping away.
From frilly socks to high income pay.
Nails always polished and heels sky high
Our girls- they are no longer naïve and shy.

Our girls-
They are assertive and confident and
stand up to be heard.
No gesture or action or statement is too absurd.
Everything we've taught them, is all put to use,
Yet not quite the way we planned it,
so we're left feeling confused.

Our girls-
They have found partners
Of every size, shape, and color.
They range from blue collar workers
to philosophy scholars.
Not quite who we hoped for,
So we put up a fight-
But our girls, our girls- they're alright.

For the first time,
In 20 something years,
Our girls will bring us to those big dreaded tears.
The ones so salty they can dry up the sea,
The ones so big they can cause a tsunami.

ON MY PERIOD

Our girls.
They've chosen their own life path and
while we are an emotional mess,
We've raised our girls to be a success.
We've raised them to have open hearts,
We've raised them to be amazing grown-ups.
We've raised them to shut down the nay-sayers,
We've raised them to be fair players.

Our girls
Look at their parents now-
We've become who we taught them never to turn in to-
Judgmental, shunning, and closed minded,
Everything our daughters don't need right now,
Well, they've found it.
The roles change now and they teach us
How to be more accepting of the world around us.

Our girls
They're not slipping away.
They're blossoming from the house we've given them to stay.
They're fearless, intelligent, and humorous too.
Their hunger for life inspires you.
Like queens on top of the highest of thrones,
They make the most of life as if they've got nothing but
Glitter in their bones.

4)

When I have my
Period
In March,
Will it be considered
A
Women's
March?

5)

I often look
At my blood
Peacefully,
Like a Rorschach blotch
Or the bottom of a finished cup of Turkish coffee,
And try to make out
What it is that my body is trying to tell me.
What ideas died inside of me
Because of tradition?
Or oppression?
Or patriarchy?
What ideas could've been breathed life in to
Had I only come in a different body?

6)

I will
Make you
Feel things
With my words.
And I will
Never
Have to touch you,
Rest assured.
But I will
Make you
Feel things
You've never felt
And you will
Be begging
To feel them all again.

7)

People run across
Manhattan streets
Like they used to run across the playground as children.
They used to run for their friends
During a game of tag
And now they run toward money,
During a game
Of get even more if you can.
Those streets of Manhattan are
Paved with sunshine
At 9 in the morning,
Soaking in all the perfume and cologne
Wore just for it.
Around 1, the streets are filled
With the allure of warm food-
Food trucks are plugged in
Like Glade in a room.
When 5 pm hits,
The sweat of the day starts to lurk in
As these ladies and gentlemen
Run back home for some din-din.

8)

Today,
We're listening to Christmas music.
It's pure and calming.
The Christmas lights are on.
They glisten on the powdered sugar
On top of the buttery pancakes.
We laugh.
We forget our troubles
For a while.
Until I sneeze and have to rush to the bathroom.

9)

As soon as you realize you don't have it,
You want it.
As soon as you realize you want it,
You must have it.
As soon as you realize you must have it,
You say you'll do anything for it.
As soon as you do anything for it,
You get it.
As soon as you get it,
You realize it's not enough.
As soon as you realize it's not enough,
You don't want it.
    - desire.

10)

And one day,
If we're lucky enough,
We'll find that peace
In a book.
We'll find it
When we're reading
A book
That smells like chalk dusk and classrooms
On a dusty green park bench in NYC
And read some words
Off a page
That resonate with us,
That hug our hearts
From within.
We'll find that peace
From a stranger
That was here once before.

11)

They call her Amor,
She's the wife of love.
She wears glitzy jewelry
And drinks red wine in the dark.
Her hair is mahogany,
Her skin is deep gold.
She's the goddess of all things
Beauty must behold.

12)

Human beings weren't just born to deliver.
They were born to take in, too.
To take life in
And deliver
Through
Words,
Language,
Ideas,
Bodies,
Life.

A cycle of processing
And producing
And delivering

A give and a take,
A take and a give.

We take life in,
We take pain in,
We take death in.

We deliver life,
We deliver pain,
We deliver death.

13)

Flashback,
Get out of my head.
You're obsessive.
I cannot focus when you're here.
You're unwanted here.
I want to leave the past where it belongs.
It pains to be reminded
Of the pain.
Flashback.
Distract yourself and think of something nice!
Like hot apple cider and candle lit relaxation.
Snow and new boots.
The sun kissing your face.
Waves! Waves on the beach.
Making cookies with mom.
Waking up to-
Flashback.
OUT!
Waking up to puppy tail wags.
Breathe.
Breathe.
Breathe.

14)

Beggars never ask women for money
When they're with another man.
They'll ask the man.
They'll ask daddy.

15)

People take diets
From food and social media.
They say cleanse your body
From the toxic it's feeding ya.
Both are avenues
For binges and purges
And then comes the need for introspective searches.
Counting calories and likes,
Looking for self-validation to be found,
But the voices inside feel so loud.
Approval is the enemy of peace
And moderation is where you'll find your release.

16)

Anger was an emotion
That was
Never accepted
For young ladies,
Unless sometimes, when you were on your period.
Ladies were never supposed to be so rude and
Get mad.
Ladies were supposed to smile and
Passively nod.
But I'm done repressing
My anger,
My fury,
The heat within my heart.
I am a lion roaring to be heard.

17)

Writing is relief.
The same way as puking
When you've had too much to drink
Or
Eat.
The same way as going to the bathroom
On your period
Feels like such a relief.
The blood rushes out.
You clean it up.
Relief.
Writing
Is relief from everything
You've been bottling up my entire life.

18)

So we study graphs and groups
More than individual people, themselves.
Always the majority.
As if numbers
Will help us unravel someone's trauma
And take their pain away.
People are simple.
We need love and care,
And someone to hold us, to hug us, to feel us.
Someone to understand us and hear us
And listen to our pain.
Someone to feel what we feel and offer a holding space,
A space of vulnerability, trust,
Warmth, and respect.
A womb.
An external womb.
When mothers have children,
They're not given a bunch of journals
And statistics.

19)

We wear our political affiliations
As accessories.
They add to our
Aesthetics
And make us
Trendy,
Hip,
Woke.
But only some can afford
To keep up with the trends.

20)

I've been watching lots of women movies lately.
You know the kind?
The ones where the women are the main characters.
The women suffer.
They pain.
They ache.
And usually few help them.
I often cry when I watch these.
I love the suffering and pain.
Because anything other than that
Is false.
Suffering is reality
And truth
And authenticity.
I
Feel
Heard.

21)

It's funny how sometimes
You have to do all the wrong things
In order to end up doing
The right thing.

22)

There was a man on the subway
Playing a drum.
His voice was calm,
His composure- well collected.
He sang
About how the drums were used
By many cultures to communicate.
How drums were used to communicate celebration
Across plantation fields.
That man
Sang his heart out.
While the woman next to him.
Stood crisply with her
Straight blonde hair
And designer purse,
Cell phone in hand and headphones in ears,
Communicating
Nothing
With
No
One.

23)

When I'm on my period,
I'm allowed to feel
All the things that are so real.
All the feelings men feel every day;
Hunger, Anger, Laziness, Play.

24)

If I have a daughter,
I will encourage her
To speak up for herself.
To be civilly disobedient if she disagrees with the law.
To be confrontational when she disagrees
with her roommate in college.
To advocate for herself to her boss.
To debate with her professor.
To disagree with her parents.
I want my daughter
To be everything that I struggled to be:
Confrontational,
Guilt-free,
Brave,
And Courageous.
And I will never,
Not ever
Put her in
Time out.
Because time's not out.
It's up.
Time's up.
#timesup

25)

I walk into the restaurant to pick up an order.
It's a heavy one- 5 bags filled with food for 17 people.
There are only men in the store.
4 construction workers eating at a table,
2 cashiers,
And 1 delivery person.
All of them ask to help me out with the bags.
I say "No."
Three ask to open the door for me.
I say "No."
Two shout out they love me.
I say "No."

26)

Can you respect those
Who have never stood up for an underdog?
For someone who maybe has trouble
standing up for themselves,
Someone who never learned how to,
Someone for which it was never safe to express that.
We can all use
Someone
To kindly stand up for us
When our legs cannot hold the weight of the pain
We're carrying.

27)

It's funny how naive we are,
How naive we can be.
We walk around as if we're not
constantly threatened by death.
But death is the wind chill on our back.
It's the silence in our head.
Death is the dark cloud looming above us.
It's the floor beneath our feet,
The heat within.
Death is always lurking,
Looking for a window to sneak in.
To rob-
To rob us from this life we were given.
Death is a thief.
Death is grief.
But, Death-
Death is also relief.

28)

Our love
Doesn't need any vacations
Or gifts.
We shrug at money
And designer brands.
Our love is a love that values
Feelings,
Emotions,
Memories,
And the fine intricacies of a life well lived,
A story well told,
The taste left in your mouth,
Rather than the caviar itself.

29)

It's funny how some men
Treat their girlfriends and wives
As royalty
But treat other women in their life
Like
Shit.
These men-
They call themselves feminists.

30)

If you were to
Grab me by my pussy right now,
Your hand
Would be a bloody mess.

31)

When I'm writing,
I feel empowered.
Seeing my feelings in front of me
Provides a cleansing-
A sort of purge
From years of repressing.
Only this feeling can compare
To the one
Of wearing heels.
    - phallic

32)

Analyze my inner demons
And feed my cleansed soul back to me.
Fill my void of desire,
And let me learn to be.
Listen to my traumas,
And out if it, create poetry.

33)

People on a stage
Have a phallic presence and ability to them.
They prance around
And put on a show for all the eyes;
For all the gazes
Watching,
Hoping,
Wishing,
They can be up there.
A holier than thou
Kind of aura and presence
That's only enlarged by desire-
The desire to be what you're enthralled with.
The desire to finally have someone give you
The same respect and attention
You were willing to give up so easily once
And to even have the audacity
To pay-
To pay to see you and
To pay-
Pay attention to.

34)

Sometimes,
When you're there for a person
After their breakup,
They will leach on to you
And think that a life with you
Will take away the pain of their own life.
They'll decide you're theirs for the taking
Because now they have shared the
most recent intimate secrets
There is to know about them.
And nobody else knows all these finite details.
But, you're not their lover-
You, too, want your own existence acknowledged.
You, too, want to be loved-
To be cherished
And accepted,
Which is why
We accept.

35)

A politically correct society
That remains repressed
Is no better than
A primitive one.

36)

So go make love to money,
While you look into my eyes-
And think of everything but me;
Watch my AP as time flies.
Diamonds galore,
Sparkles in our eyes.
You tell me I'm beautiful
And I wonder if it still applies.
Since all you seemed to be focused on
Is all my damn armor
And even then, I'm basic enough
To call you a real charmer.

37)

People who take advantage of people
Feel some kind of
Entitlement over them.
Some form of power over them.
And those who allow
Others
To take advantage of them
Feel that they are not deserving of something
More.

38)

Freud said he never figured out
What it was that women want.
I wrote this book so people know
What women want
While on their period.
Interesting
How it's all pretty much the same.
We always want what we want,
And we don't even know the clarity of it all.
The only difference is that
Our wants are amplified during that time-
A reminder of who we are,
And what our sex means to us.
And what sex means to us.
And what we want because of our sex.
Because of the predetermined societal structures,
We have a desire
To do and to be
Better.

39)

And five years from now,
I hope you hold on to my love
Like the pain of the waves
Crashing above.
Feel the shards of the sand
As you let go of my hand,
Running after me,
Solitary.

40)

Slowly, slowly,
Hands that know me.
Eyes that undress me,
Touches that caress me.
Lips that taste me,
Legs that chase me.
Fingers that mend me,
Knees that will bend for me.

41)

She comes around,
Lays herself on the ground,
Pushes him out-
Says, "I can't take it right now."
He lays next to her,
Braces her body and curls
On the carpet besides her-
He tries to try harder.
He brushes her hair,
To show her he cares.
He soothes her with ease,
You'd think this was a breeze.
"So heavenly and divine,
A man that is all mine."
She says that
And she cries
Tears that are never ready to say goodbye.

42)

Everyone wants to say something clever,
Always looking for a synonym,
A spicy word,
Something to shatter.
A glass ceiling or heel-
It's the art of the deal.

43)

I have so many cravings while on my period:
Milk chocolate covered pretzels,
Chocolate chip cookie dough ice cream,
Nutella,
Being a mother,
Dark chocolate covered pomegranate chews,
Dipping my whole bloody body in a pool,
Egg and cheese on a toasted bagel,
Half-baked warm brownies with a scoop of vanilla ice cream,
Skipping the gym for a week,
Aged asiago cheese with grapes and pickles,
Macedonian hazelnut balls,
Holding a baby of my own,
Trail Mix,
Ferrero Rocher,
Ketchup,
A fruit salad with whipped cream on top,
Having a Kim Kardashian body,
Honey BBQ ribs dripping with sauce,
Skipping work and school for a week,
Vanilla coffee from an upscale coffee shop,
A matcha latte,
Ice cold water,
Sleeping the whole week.
But I've never craved
Anything as much
As publishing a
Book of my own.

44)

The world will break me
And words will shatter me
But you will hold me
And make me feel
Home.

45)

I get the allure of Versace perfume,
The way the fragrance fills up a room.
I understand the appeal of beautiful heels-
They click on Manhattan pavement and give you the feels.
I was never one to care much
About the oh so classy Kate Spade clutch.
But sometimes, I like to indulge
In the things that bulge.

46)

I feel
I feel too much
I haven't written a poem in
A
While
Now
Because it's too difficult to
Come to terms with my emotions.
It hurts to re-feel what I felt
Just to write
What I want to get across.
I feel anger
I feel pain
I feel
I feel
I feel
All
Too
Much.

47)

People
Used to hunt
For food.
They used to make maps
Of where to go to get some meat.
Now, people hunt
For restaurants.
They use Google Maps
To find the best brunch spots
For bottomless mimosas.
People used to
Shoot
Animals so they can eat to live.
People now
Shoot
Pics of their food because they live to eat.

48)

Ave Maria,
Here I am on your couch.
Let me tell you all my sins,
I have the courage to come now.

Ave Maria,
Please listen to me.
I'll lay for you right here,
I'm at your mercy.
Ave Maria,
I know my guilt is a shame.
I've come to you for punishment
But you give me understanding again.
Ave Maria,
Please, hit me!
The way it has been done before,
Repeat the damage for a hefty fee.
Ave Maria
How you disappoint me so.
I'm asking you to shame me!
To slap me down to my toes!

Oh Maria!
Why are you starving me?
I'm starved of the pain and the agony.
Maria, Maria
Who am I without my pain?
This existential questioning
Is driving me insane.
A hysteric at heart,

ON MY PERIOD

My shrink is the dart.
Existence is pain, Maria.
I was in pain, Maria.
If I was pain and pain is existence,
I only existed through pain.
Oh Maria,
Ave, Ave,
I've got to rebuild myself now.
Open the cage for the doves right now.
Take the scars off of my flesh somehow,
Feed my starving stomach some love and bow,
You can take a bow I said.
I asked for an ill life, you showed me death.
You gave me reasons
To separate,
To separate from this wretched hate-
This wretched hate for my own life.
My identity was pain
And pain brought on guilt and shame,
You took my hand,
Healed me soul,
Paved the way
For me to grow.
They hail Mary,
While I hail a cab.
They pray to God,
I lay on my analyst's bed.
They're forgiven of sins
And I'm forgiven of pain
Lovers of life,
Let us begin again.

49)

We're obsessed with freezing time.
We capture emotions in snaps,
Memories in drives and clouds,
Artwork in frames,
Life in taxidermy,
Reality in shows,
Nature in the glass enclosures at the
Museum of Natural History,
Death in the ground.
We horde life and death
And everything in between.
We horde happiness,
We horde pain.
And we're sick because of it.
Because we're sick in the present,
We keep going back to these memories of the past,
And become anxious about being mindful of the past
In the future.
It's almost as if we know
That's never bound to happen.

50)

Poverty struck families,
Single mothers,
And dead-beat fathers.
Trauma, abuse, and neglect-
Substances start to have an effect.
The endless hustle never ends,
Jail is a vacation;
You lose all your friends.
The state provides
A home you almost lost-
Electricity, food, and water
At no cost.
You sit in the box-
It's a time out,
Yet somehow it feels like no bother.
The state becomes
A surrogate father.

51)

Body on top of body
Body under body
Body inside of body
Baby
Baby inside of body
Body inside of body
Body out of body
Embodied body

52)

So she'll be kind,
And a bit too talkative,
And send gifts,
And cards,
And be interested in your interests,
And lose herself in you-
All because she's already so lost.
She craves the love,
The attention,
Because she never got it at home.
So, she'll try it with someone else.
And from afar,
It seems so sad.
On the outside looking in,
It looks alarming.
But it feels so familiar.
It's a vicious cycle
Of admiring someone who
Admires someone else too much
To care.
So, when you find someone who admires you,
You ignore them
Because you are still after
The love you'll never get.

53)

Gifts
Suck.
People watch you open them.
And you can never genuinely hate a gift.
Because that's rude.
And you have to say thank you-
Even when the gift isn't thoughtful.
There's no consent in gift-giving,
Unless you don't accept it at all,
Which is even more rude.
And you have to give them a gift
Next time
Because if you don't, that's also so rude.
And also,
Gifts hold leverage over you
Sometimes.
And then you think about money.
And you associate yourself with a number.
Another number.
Like the number on the scale.
And so, you amount to nothing more than money
And body.
A body that accepts.
A body that consumes.
A body that costs money to maintain.
A profitable body.

54)

So
I can't curse
Or fart
Or burp
Or dress ugly
Or not brush my hair
Or be disobedient
Because I'm a lady.
If being a lady means being less of a human
And
Being a man means embodying humanity,
I don't want to be a lady.
But they say I won't get married.
If being married means being more confined-
Confined
Con Fined
Fined
Charged
Guilty
Crime…
It's a crime to confine me.
So, they say,
Find yourself a man
That will still love you when you
Curse
And fart
And burp
And dress ugly

Elena Petrovska

And not brush your hair
And disobey him
Because he does not own you.
So, society shouldn't
Confine me even more
By telling me
That I can't marry him.
Because if so,
I will cry
And scream-
No.
I will ugly cry- LOUD!
And nasty scream-
The kind of scream that will make your skin crawl
And throw a fucking tantrum because
I'm a lady.
And ladies are hysterics.
And so maybe then you'll accept me.
Because at least
I'll be doing
What I'm supposed to
And fitting in to the tiny space
That I'm supposed to fit into.

55)

Men don't respect
You
When you tell them
That you're in a relationship.
They take it as
An invitation for competition.

56)

In the service industry,
Whatever that may be,
People pay to use up your body.
Servers, doctors,
Therapists, lawyers.
Chefs, teachers,
Beauticians, lawn mowers.
You're a substance
For people to use
When they have nothing left to abuse.

57)

But the chains
Don't matter
If you've got feet to run.

58)

I tried to punch the
Space of air
In front of me,
But I was just punching like a girl.
He came in front of me
With gloves
And I started punching like a damn man.
"Maybe all you needed was something to punch,"
He said.

59)

Anorexic bodies
Are wire hangers.
And a monkey
And a baby
Prefer cloth mommies
To wire mommies.

60)

You don't pay for the product.
Nine times out of ten,
When you pay,
It's not about the drugs,
Or the food,
Or the overpriced drink.
It's about the moment-
Stepping away from a busy atmosphere
And going somewhere calmer,
And quieter,
And indulging in something together.
It's about the atmosphere around you-
The dimly lit lighting that illuminates your skin,
Or the live music dancing into your body,
Or the change in external location
That shakes things up-
Takes you away
And provides an escape.
It's never about the substance.
The substance is an excuse-
A substitute for words.
Because it's easier to say.
And then,
When people disappoint you
And leave,
You start associating the substance to the person.
The mac and cheese with the grandmother.
The pinot grigio with your lover.

ON MY PERIOD

The cigarettes with your aunt.
And you miss them
So, you smoke,
Drink,
Eat
Yourself to death.
Because loneliness is a curse
And you just want to be held.

61)

So there's this guy,
Right?
And I love him, I love him, I love him.
He reminds me of my father-
Not all the things.
But some.
When I get mad at one,
I get mad at the other.
And when I get mad at myself,
I get mad at my mother.
    - Oedipus

62)

I feel hungover-
But I didn't drink.
I feel wasted,
Because I can't think.
I'm a mess.
I'm on fire.
Everything's chaotic-
I'm walking on a thin wire.
I want to scream
"NO!" to everyone.
I want to leave and just run.
I've never been taught how to disobey.
So, by everyone else's rules- I play.
I'm red,
I am blood.
I want to say No.
I want to explode.
I want to be mad.
I want to break rules.
I want to be me.
I want
To
Just
Be
F
R
E
E.

63)

The fate of the world is crumbling;
People trying to mess with nature.
Let it happen,
Let it be.
Golden tulips, purple seas.
Crunchy acorns, crispy leaves.
A tiny lash on your silken pillowcase.
A lady walking with such grace.
Softened sunshine, wispy rain,
Nurture my body
With your plane.

64)

Don't take my poetry
Personally.
It's a mental work of art.
An intellectual orgasm of some sort.
Don't take my poetry
Personally
And ask me to make things sound
Nicer and more polite.
You wouldn't ask an artist
To blur some things out,
Am I not right?
Don't take my poetry
Personally,
And
If you ask me to censor,
I won't.

65)

Groupchat.
1 girl, 3 guys.
She puts down the guys-
Stomps her heel into their hands.
They like it.
They all like her comments.
She finally likes herself.
Domination.
   - external validation

66)

We have so much retaliation coiled up.
People making things difficult
Because that's how it was for them.
People handing out abuse like candy
Because they have so many leftovers
from their own childhood.
We accumulate so much pain
And instead of throwing it in the garbage,
We horde and
Purge it all.
So, the pain and abuse go around
Like a carousel.

67)

I feel spread so t h i n
Like butter on warm toast,
Soft rain on concrete,
Bold lipstick on lips.
People take from me
What they need
And when needed.
An hour here,
Another there.
I'm finding it more and more difficult to care
About myself.
I feel unreal.
I peel my skin just to feel.
I see the blood- it feels like pain.
Easier to feel pain than shame
Or anger,
Fear,
Guilt, and
Love.
I start to shatter
Because I'm so worn out.
Life is flooding from my face.
I fall like a ballerina with nothing to taste.
I can't even sweat,
Cry,
Or smile.
All the pieces of me are worn out and dry.
If you put the portions

ON MY PERIOD

Of pieces left
Back together,
You'll find that
I should probably feel better.
I've always wanted to be thin-
Well, now I'm the thinnest.
No room in my body for myself-
I'm the illest.

68)

Let me vomit in your mouth
All the things I can't spit out.
All the pain, fear, and disgust,
I've kept inside me- bottled up.
Let me spit out this wrecked mess.
All the bacteria, all the damn stress.
Let me create chaos in you,
Let me show you my masterpiece in the loo.
Look at my glory- look at my pain.
My choice of medium is quite insane.
Look at me and what I just made.
Now flush it all down- for I don't get paid.
A temporary unframed work of art.
Made in seconds, then gone in the dark.
All that's left of this whole disgrace
Are the small red busted blood clots on my face.
Look in my eyes and you will see
All the ways your words continue to punish me.
All the shame and guilt you made me feel-
All the trauma is quite real.
I've lost the words to express my anger-
I feel abandoned like a child in a manger.
So, I use my body to show you
The ways you inspired me to hate myself too.

69)

Some girls learn,
At an early age
That they can soften men
With a smile.
And sometimes,
They carry it over
With them
To adulthood.
What may look like naivety
To some,
Is actually taking advantage of the patriarchy
To others.
Do you still think I'm flirting with you?
   - just trying to get a discount

70)

Borderline hysteria.
Why isn't that a thing?
Hysterics are conflicted with their sexuality,
While borderlines are conflicted with everything.
But what if you're both?
What if both life and death
Are something you loathe?

71)

I feel submissive,
They make me crueler.
I just want to write,
But nobody's buying.
I just want to write,
But people are saying
That they want someone to hear them out,
They want someone to watch them pout
And vent
And cry about life.
So, they'll pay someone to hear them in real time.
They'll pay to be heard,
But they won't pay to listen
To the struggles people have in similar events.
They won't pay a museum,
Bookstore,
Or musician,
Because they need to feel alive
More than they need to feel like they fit in.

72)

I feel insane
In the University.
I'm becoming more vicious,
Like a ravenous lion searching for prey.
I have a hunger for the professor's approval
And all these classmates
Are my siblings.
So, we cry,
And we scream,
Hoping to be heard.
"Look at me, I'm smart!"
"Look at me, look at me, look at me!"
It's survival of the fittest
And we'd do anything
Just to get in to
The Debt Club.
We'd do anything to get in to
A club where we feel like we
Always owe someone something.
But what do we owe to
Ourselves?

73)

I remember singing in Pre-K,
That I've got the whole world in my hands.
I look around now and realize
Everyone's got it in their hands.
    - technology

74)

I have always questioned men
Who buy flowers for their wives
Every time they pick them up from the airport.
If the gesture is done over and over,
Does it mean anything anymore?
Do men do this because they see it on TV
Or because they think it's what men are supposed to do?
I have never asked for flowers.
In fact, I really don't like receiving them.
They are temporary and they die.
I want to be picked up at the airport,
Not with flowers,
But with arms and words that fill my heart,
Whispers in my ear that give my arms chills,
That purse open my lips,
That make me dizzy.
Words that fill the air around us that make
The rest of the people at airport stand still
For a minute or so,
Appreciating the beauty
We exude,
The life we express,
The more permanent kind
Of (de) flower(ing).
Love.

75)

A teacher can open your mind without ever touching it.
A lover can hold your heart without squeezing it.
An instructor can shape your body without reaching it.
A therapist can touch you with just words.
And a stranger can break everything again
With
Just
One
Touch.

76)

He's the
Head of the family.
"Which head?"
I ask.

77)

When they're on their period,
Some women
Wait outside and shed their egg
While people inside celebrate eggs, life, and rebirth.

78)

Her dad hasn't called her
Beautiful
Since she started liking boys.

79)

All my sisters are thinner than me,
All my sisters are prettier than me,
All my sisters are more loved than me,
They all say.
    - *Who's right?*

80)

I don't like history,
Because there's a lot of conflict,
And wars,
And people are constantly fighting over territory,
And superiority,
And patriarchy v. matriarchy.
I don't like history
Because if we focus too much on it,
We don't give people a chance to grow,
And improve,
And change.
Quite frankly,
Does that hit too close to home?

81)

People's bodies will act out in ways
That embody their emotions:
Not eating
Vomiting
Binging
Skin picking
Hair pulling
Smoking
Drinking
Drugging
Arguing
Cheating
Lying
Stealing.
We're all a bunch of
Hurt children
Acting out our emotions
Because they're too painful to express
With logical words of reality.

82)

Mama-
Hold me as I cry.
It's been a while since you've held me
The way you used to.
We've hurt each other,
It's part of life.
But let's forgive.
You know that I love you.
I want to feel your warmth,
Your love.
I know your body as you know mine.
I've been deep inside you.
Don't pull away-
Don't cut the cord.
Losing your love is not something
I can emotionally afford.
I need you,
I miss you,
I love you.
You're not losing me.
Emotional ties are stronger than physical ones, you see.

83)

Maybe women are so
Territorial
Over the kitchen
Because they finally
Get to be in control of
Putting something
Inside of
A man's body
For once.

84)

We find
People,
Places,
And ideas
That
Shelter our relationships
And allow them to
Flourish.

85)

Smother me.
Mother me.
I need someone to nurture me.
Water me.
Feed me.
Engage with me.
Get engaged to me.
Play with me.
Stay with me.
Be mine.

86)

People despise me,
I'm an overachiever.
But I don't do it to be better than anyone.
I do it because I never get approval.
And when I do, it's never enough.
And I want more.
I don't do it to compete.
I do it to feel complete.
There's so much pain
In never feeling
Good enough.
They don't see
How this hole in me
Is never satisfied.
    - Addicted

87)

Confinement fulfills the desire of comfort.
4 walls,
4 walls.
Empirical answers.
A solid answer and statement.
Comfort in numbers,
Comfort in pain.
4 walls-
A womb.
Silence.
Always silence.
Passive.
Pass through life.
Pass through the womb.
Pass into life.
We crave the passivity of it all.
We build up walls
To create the womb
We crave to be in yet again.
What is there to pass through
If there isn't a wall?
We like the walls.
We miss the silence.
We become the silence.
We don't speak up.
We enmesh
Into the walls.
Into the womb.

Elena Petrovska

Skin into skin.
We become the womb.
We become the wall.
We cry into life.
We cry all throughout life.
We cry as we exit life.
We cry.

88)

When I hit,
I punch away my own pain
And I get rewarded with,
"Good job, now do it again!"
I punch and I jab,
I kick and I curse.
I'm a hell of a women.
And I feel stronger than
When just wearing a skirt.

89)

Pick.
It's eating away at me.
I pick,
My skin is a battleground.
Blood.
Yes,
I'm alive.
Pain.
Good.
Better out than in.
Let it bleed.
Soak.
Gone.
No- it's back.
Caught me red handed.
Bye-bye emotions.
Hello Band-Aids.
Pick, pick, pick.
The problem is me.
I pick.
Can't blame anyone for making me want to pick.
They all tell me, "Stop it, stop it!"
And I throw that right back at them.
Stop it?
I'll stop when you do.

90)

Some days, it's red,
Like the Sahara at sunset- soaking in
every last bit of sunshine.
Some days, it's brownish red,
Like the skin of a pomegranate that my mom
used to buy me when I was in high school.
Some days, it's purplish red,
Like a fallen, crispy autumn leaf, withering
at the edges and slowly fading.
Some days, it's pink,
Like the blueberry mush my sister would make
with her hands when she was a baby.
Some days, it's bright red,
Like the cherry syrup I'd force down
my throat when I was sick.
All days, it was kind of pretty.
I bleed.

91)

If you want to be a poet,
You've got to be petty.
You have to look at an object,
Or a person,
Or a place,
And start romanticizing it.
It could be a murder,
But the way the police headlights shined upon the blood
Could be beautiful.
Or perhaps,
A woman saved someone.
It can't be a man as the hero, though,
Because poets are progressive.
Poets carry their tools everywhere they go.
Their eyes, their ears, their imagination, and their tears.
They have the license to feel
And to make you feel.
You can watch someone give birth
Or you can contract words yourself,
Push them out of you
And give life to a new baby
That can grow into a whole story later on.
But for now, it's just a thought.
It's just a poem.
That's because poets have way too many ideas.
Their minds work faster than their hands.
When a poet sits down to write,
It's like they're in a race against time.

ON MY PERIOD

They'll think of an idea on the subway
And take out their phone to jot down a note,
Only to notice a couple interacting on the subway,
Genuinely laughing and cuddling.
Poets will end up in another borough
Just because they were too busy watching
A poem being written right in front of their own eyes.
Then they'll write another poem
About getting lost.
Poets are petty like that.

92)

She pulls out a pen
"This is my nice pen," she says.
Nice?
I notice myself judging.
I ask myself-
How many "nice" pens
Have I pulled out
That people have smirked at?
But then I think of my mentor who said
She collects people like pens.
And then I think about how I
Collect mentors.

93)

I'm starting to nurture myself
And it feels so...new.
I'm gentle with my body.
I take breaks when I need to as I exercise.
I pay attention to cravings and desires.
I compare myself- to myself.
I sometimes forget to compare myself.
I stop counting numbers.
I get rid of my scale.
I challenge myself,
But I have realistic expectations.
I water myself, I feed myself.
I indulge.
I take myself out.
I go on walks.
I dance and sing.
I let myself cry.
Some days,
I'll argue with myself
And wear myself down.
But as with any relationship,
I'll apologize and mean it and move on.

94)

Maybe,
Instead of being what we eat,
We are how we eat.
We're impulsive-
Our thoughts anxiously flood in and
we can't slow down our mind.
Our hands anxiously open groceries and
we can't slow down our...mind.
We're restrictive-
We punish ourselves with hateful self-talk and remarks.
We deprive ourselves of fuel and energy.
We're compensating-
We make up for punishing ourselves by
being kind- and then, mean, again.
We make up for depriving ourselves by eating
a lot- and then running for 3 hours.
We're messy-
We make a mess in our mind as we try to ration and reason.
We make a mess in our plate as we
pick out what we really want.
We're organized-
We plan everything out because order makes us calm.
We plan out all our meals because we thrive on stability.
We're mindful-
Our body and mind is at ease as we take
in the world one breath at a time.
Our body and mind is at ease as we take in
our nourishment one bite at a time.

ON MY PERIOD

The day we shift from seeing
Eating habits, rather than
Body shape and size as a metaphor for who we are
Is the day we'll begin to have
Better relationships with food,
Our bodies,
And our minds.
We're not just what we eat-
We're where we eat
And when we eat
And why we eat
And how we eat.

95)

Sweet smells of frozen sugar mixed with heavy diesel,
The sun hitting our faces at just the right angles,
Hot sweat coating our overheated bodies.
The smell of sunshine invigorates me.
The winter sadness is passed and gone.
The smell of summer turns me on.

96)

A poem is metaphoric
For life, itself.
You start out with a general outlook on an idea
And as you go on,
Sometimes other things pop up
And your poem takes a turn
In a different direction.
But you roll with the punches
And you end up with a final product, anyway.
A period is poetic,
For life, itself.
There's inconsistency in
Color, amount, length, and pain.
And you roll with yourself
And become comfortable with
The inconsistency.
Poetry and Periods.
Inconsistent-
Yet artistic.

97)

Sometimes,
I let go of all the bottled-up rage
That I hid for so long in this delicate body.
I turn on a light that's only known darkness
And since it's only known darkness,
It lights up with all the bottled-up electricity.
It fills up a whole building
And penetrates through every crack.
My anger cannot be controlled once it's released.
It doesn't turn off
Until everyone's eyes are blinded
And filled with fear.
Who knew
A tiny little lightbulb can fuck up
A whole building?
The silence hears echoes of fear.
The light shuts them all up.
I've enlightened them.

98)

I knew why
I enjoyed the smell
Of that
Juicy Couture
Perfume
So much
That my parents bought for me.
It smelled as heavenly as
Those rose infused
Baklava treats
I once tried
And loved so much.
I think I enjoyed
Eating and
Smelling like roses more
Than I enjoyed receiving them.

99)

My love smells like sin.
To people that have never been caught in
This type of love,
My god, it fills me up
To the brim, you intoxicate.
My skin
Glows as you
Call me beautiful.

100)

The lawyer's daughter is a shrink.
The two fields can overlap.
There are law journals and psychology journals;
Legal laws and scientific laws;
Dissenting opinions and dissenting studies.
Sometimes,
When law meets therapy,
You can have a well-rounded dyad.
You can have justice.
You can have liberty.
And freedom-
Freedom to be.

101)

I'm sitting like a statue,
Reading about patient attunement research.
I'm sitting like a statue,
Like a catatonic woman,
Typing up a poem.
Numbers scare me-
They alienate me from humanity.
I've never felt more alone.
Everyone's talking about measuring.
Measuring,
Measuring,
Measuring nonverbal synchrony.
What's my nonverbal synchrony?
I'm sitting like a pissed off patient,
Dissociating,
Crying inside,
Suffering.
And yet, I'm here
Wondering why it is
That people want to measure everything-
Even poems.
5-7-5
I weep.
I just want to write.
I just want to connect.
How can we be attuned when we feel so alone?

102)

I go through poetic periods
Of life-
Literally.
I think I can't wait to get my period now-
Not just to confirm my lack of motherhood,
But also, to confirm my ability to be alive.
To write!
To feel alive while writing.
I crave this period where I allow myself to be free.
To bleed freely-
From the inside out.
From my body to paper-
Pad or online notebook.
I've given myself the gift
Of finding art in my pain.
I think Nietzsche and Freud would've been proud.
But even so,
I'm proud!
And that's the only approval that should matter.
Should, I said.

103)

I've learned to give birth
To something
At the same time as
Confirming I'm not pregnant.

104)

My anxiety mimics
Hunger pangs.
I feel it in my chest-
I'm burning up.
I feel it in my stomach-
It's pulling my heart down.
I feel it in my head-
A pounding gavel.
Judging, judging, always judging.
Anxiety.
Hunger.
Anxiety feeds my hunger.
Hunger feeds my anxiety.
Food issues.
Hunger.
Anxiety.
I eat,
Yet I'm starving.
I long for something more.

105)

Are we synchronizing with Mother Nature?
When it's cold, we're bitter.
When it's hot, we're warm.
When it's rainy, we weep.
When it snows, we play.
When it's windy, we're flaky.
We're attuned with Nature.
We're at one.

106)

I want to get lost in your music,
I want to get lost in your love.
I want to feel your love beating in my heart,
Like the beat of concert drums.
I want to throw my hands up-
I want to sing along-
I want our words to blend into one,
One fucking good song.

107)

Let's make women's bodies phallic, they said.
Let's make their butt the testes
And their erect spine and back the phallus.
Let's make women the most
Phallic part of men.

108)

Sing me a song
Of a white veil brushing up on the shore,
Right at the cusp where the water meets the sand.
Sing me a song of his sweet cologne
Brushing over her hand.
Sing me that song they've forbidden to be sung,
The one that forced wedding bells to be rung.
I can never picture myself wearing white-
Sing me a song of a woman
Willing to fight.

109)

There's still a
Hunger involved
In the chase to be thin.

110)

Good, Bad
Right, Wrong
Love, Hate
Bi, Polar
Stop, Thinking
This, Way
Because, It's
Driving, Me
In, Sane.

111)

Loud silence.
Worse than quiet noise.
It cannot be ignored nor shut out.
Ears too weak to block this out.
When we're in pain,
When we're helpless,
When we ask and ask and ask and ask,
But there is no answer-
Silence.
Painful, dreadful, and nothing.
Nothingness is incomprehensible for living beings.
Defeat.
We are left in the dark,
Under the earthly soil of the Earth,
After a brisk evening rain,
After a drying sun.
We are left,
Attached to the Earth
In a wooden womb-
Attachment begins and ends life.
Tied to the umbilical cord of flesh,
Tied to the umbilical cord of the roots of a tree.
In a wooden womb-
Left to absorb the rain, the sun, the snow, the love.
Left to absorb the future of the world.
We are alone
In silence.
Nothing but the screams of silence.

112)

And so, I find myself
Playing tug of war with myself.
I find myself arguing with myself.
My Superego and Id are at odds
And I've spent too many train rides
Crying in front of strangers.
But it's New York so nobody asks what's wrong
And I prefer it that way,
Because how would I even begin to explain
Something that breaks me apart over and over again.
I argue and argue hours at a time
With myself and it's almost out of line.
Love has no scale and I can't give up either end.
I find myself losing either way.
I find myself crying all day.
They say I caused them so much pain,
And I wish I could say that for me, it's the same.
But I can't pull an emotional trigger,
Because I know that the guilt only seeps in deeper.
As time passes, it eats away at you
And I love them too much
To make them feel guilty too.
So, I hold on to both ends,
It's me in the middle
And I wish I could just-
Pull both ends together
And have them meet-
Tie up a knot
And drop the circle by my feet.

113)

How can I
Pick myself up
And dust myself off
When it takes me at least three days
To recover from each fall?

114)

A train slugs by
Brightly lit New York City lights;
She thinks of her sisters.
The memories of them twinkle in front of her;
Sweaty bike rides and heavy tears,
Bouncing on the trampoline and making them meals,
Stopping by neighborhood fairs at night
And ridding on roller coasters with lights; so bright!
She hugs her eyelids together
And dreams
Future gatherings with little kids,
Nieces and nephews run ahead.
She licks her lips...
A salty taste.
Nostalgia and dreaming
Puts her in a daze.

115)

People pay for dead sea
Face masks,
But I use tears...
It's the newest craze.
People pay to go and see
The red sea,
But for me,
It's right in the bathroom.

116)

A musician carries their instrument on their back,
An anorexic carries their struggle on their body.
A lawyer wears their confidence and class,
A fashion designer wears their fancy dress.
A homeless person wears their wear and tear
And a hairdresser shows off their hair.
But me-
You cannot tell.
I hide both pain and success so well.

117)

She used pistachio shells
As bowls for Barbie dolls.
She played with my sisters
And they even shared clothes.
She read her writing aloud to me
And surprised me with her vocabulary.
She left the world in great pain-
The last I saw her, she was entering the train.

118)

I think it's funny what love can make us do.
Love can make us threaten lives,
Love can cut relationship ties.
Love can heal deep set pain,
Love can make you live again.

119)

People rebel-
People always rebel.
If not against their parents,
Then against their spouse.
If not against their spouse,
Then against their boss.
If not against their boss,
Then against their government.
If not against their government,
Then against their country.
If not against their country,
Then against themselves.
If not against themselves,
Then there is no change.
If there is no change,
Then who are we?

120)

I love quiet men.
It unleashes a side of me that I'd love to see again.
A quiet man
Is an uncharted terrain.
Let me water those fields and
Awaken the grain.
Quiet men don't flaunt.
I like a little mystery-
I don't need a show-off.
I like my men quiet.
It makes more room for me.
I want to be the loud one-
I want other women to see.
Quiet men are mysterious
And charming.
They hide a lot in their silence.
And me-
I'm a lion, at heart.
When I roar,
I want someone to hear.
And when I purr,
I want someone to hold me near.
    - Leo

121)

Is it still equality
When we're getting paid the same, but
All the work falls into my hands?
My maternal instincts kick in.
I need to take care of people.
I need to be there for people.
I need to do what he's not doing.
I get paid the same,
But I'm picking up his slack.
I'm not breaking glass ceilings-
I'm breaking my own back.
Have you seen two men working together?
The work is usually equally split.
Have you seen a man and woman and
a man working together?
The woman takes the hit.

122)

Mothers-
Stop cleaning up after your son.
Show him how the laundry should be done.
Fathers-
Stop telling him which girls to date,
Or that he has to run to home plate.
Sisters-
You can protect your brother, too,
And give back to him as he has done to you.
Brothers-
Don't compare each other,
Hug, share, and love one another.
Mothers,
Ask him to help you around the house-
Ask him to do the dishes,
Not just to kill the mouse.
Show him how to make a nice meal,
Ask him every day, "How do you feel?"

123)

Dorm.
Shit.
So much shit.
They smear it, they don't clean it.
We must be a parent and tell them to clean their shit!
Money.
They complain about the money- the cost of living.
It's not their money- it's their parents'.
Babies.
Or the protection against them.
Condoms and pills galore.
Penis'.
Drawn everywhere,
So we add a vagina next to each one.
Shit=Money=Babies=Penis
   - phallocentric

124)

When you're ready to publish a book,
You just know it.
You feel it deep within your bones.
You feel the contractions.
And the water breaks.
Your tear-flooded heart bursts again.
Push- push- push the words out,
Push the pain out,
Push your feelings out,
Push the truth out,
Push life out.
Breathe life into thoughts,
Breathe life into ideas,
Breathe life into what was never spoken about,
Breathe life into what almost died;
But hang on
For just a bit longer,
To give you a chance to breathe life back into it.
When you're ready to publish a book,
The water breaks.
It all breaks loose.
You're flooded.
Your brain is flooded and you just gotta get it out there,
So that it's no longer inside of you,
Sucking you from the inside out.
It may suck you from the outside in, though
And leave you dry.
But at least you can watch it grow

Elena Petrovska

From all that it sucked out of you.
You can watch it grow and develop
And be with other people
And grow and develop and influence them.
But you gotta let it go.
For now,
It is bigger than you.
Let it grow.
When you're ready to publish a book,
It comes out
Whether you want it to or not.

125)

Make US Love Again.
Let's learn to love again.
Let's learn to make love again,
To hug again,
To kiss again.
Let's learn to listen again,
To feel again.
To breathe each other in again.
Let's learn to be kind again.
Be mine again.
Let's believe in love again.

126)

Breathe me in,
As I breath you.
Share my life with me too.
I'll take in what you breathe out,
There's something so romantic about
Mouth to mouth.

127)

Word play.
Play on words.
Words on play.
Play with words.
Words in play.
Play out words.
Words out of play.
Mold words,
Like clay.

128)

I answer my cat calls
As I do to my emails.
Cat calls,
Fan calls.
Give me a break
And get the director to
Call cut!

129)

To look at people
You find to be dimes,
Perfect 10s-
Chads and Staceys.
To look at skinny people,
With perfect teeth,
And amazingly beautiful features.
To look at people who won
The genetic lottery.
And discard them
And hate them
Because you want to be them,
Is objectifying them.
Is dismissing them out of spite
And never getting to know them as a person.
You may hate them,
But what if you like them?

130)

I've got anxiety
And anxiety has me.
Together we make
A pretty nice
Family.

131)

Sometimes, Death gets a little lonely
And tugs at Life's sleeve.
"Give me some love," he begs.
"Not tonight." she says.
"Maybe tomorrow," she adds.
Death gets a little bothered and he calls her name out again.
"Please, I'm tired of being so lonely," he weeps.
"Give me just a little bit of love," he asks again.
"Fine. I'll give you some love," she says.
She looks at her array of dolls.
Some she loves more than others.
Death looks really lonely.
His eyes are droopy; they almost look black.
He hasn't slept for days and needs some company.
She picks her finest doll.
"This one's really nice," she says.
"You'll like this one a lot," she adds.
Death livens up with joy.
His face floods with color.
And so it goes.
When Death is sad, Life tries to cheer him up.
She shares her toys
Because she knows she'll get them back.
They won't always look the same
Because he likes to change them up.
But she gets them back.
And so the dolls are shared back and forth
Between Life and Death

Elena Petrovska

And they spend some time here and some time there.
Never with the same dolls, though, because
sometimes Life gets lonely too.
And when Life misses someone,
Death gives them back to her
And then she'll change them up and
hand them back to Death.
Life and Death.
They share.
They share, and they never keep any
doll with them for too long.
The dolls-
They're always in between.
Getting passed from Life to Death;
From Death to Life.

132)

Men love heels.
They love envisioning something so hard
And powerful on a woman.
And to be fair,
Heels lift women up too.
And sometimes,
There's a change in perspective
And we're not forced to look up at men-
Heels even the playing field.

133)

Sometimes, funerals are prettier than weddings.
People bring their egos with them to weddings.
They're not happy for the couple because
they're envious they don't have a partner.
They're not happy in general because the
couple isn't the same as them.
They're not happy because their partner was
chosen for them when it was their turn.
People bring their guilt with them to funerals.
Guilty for causing them pain.
Guilty for thinking badly of them.
Guilty for being too focused on things that
don't matter at the end of one's life.
Funerals are forgiving.
Weddings are reason to hold grudges.
If we celebrated life more,
Maybe death wouldn't be so painful.
But then again,
What's so pretty about guilt?

134)

I feel the weight of the tissue
Soaked with tears of pain.
I think death sucks
Because it's not tangible.
You can't feel the body you'll never feel again.
Can't see the goodbye you'll never get to say.
Can't hear the voice that's going to disappear.
Can't smell death coming.
Can't get a taste of what nothingness is like.
You have to give the body back to the earth.
You feel like you've stolen moments with the person,
But they're not yours.
They're not even their own.
Their body is just their home.
They leave the body they live in.
They borrow the clothes to live in,
And then slip away-
For good.
Except it feels bad.

135)

Why don't you give me a chance?
Whisper your darkness to me.
Let it carry over to who I'm about to see.
Paint me a picture of your grim past-
This is the only way to make our brightness dance.
Cover me with your depth,
Pull me out with your love.
I'll reward you with sunshine,
Until you're warm enough.
    - avoidant

136)

As a woman,
I infantilize myself.
I blame my womanhood
On getting lost,
On not being well versed in reading maps,
On not driving well.
I handicap myself.
I can't handle technology,
Or taxes,
Or sports.
But I'm learning
That maybe these are just things
That don't interest me.
I'd rather explore.
I'd rather communicate with people for directions.
I'd rather walk.
I'd rather write.
I'd rather take my time.
I'd rather bake.

137)

Sometimes death awakens
Our ability to live.
Sometimes it takes a little pain
To cause an earthquake
Within our body.
To shake us up a bit,
To awaken our spirit,
Our soul.
Our light is illuminated most
In the darkest places.

138)

When I drink,
I feel a thirst for numbness.
I sip to feel nothing and just live full Id.
I taste nothingness on my tongue as I become
Unenchanted by the taste of nothing.
I want to stop feeling,
To stop thinking,
To stop overthinking.
I dance.
I dance without limit
And feel no pain as the backs of my shoes
Rub against my feet, bringing them to bleed.
I bleed but I'm laughing.
I smile and I'm not afraid
To keep sipping this holy potion,
That stops me from going insane.

139)

I guess I feel like I was robbed
Of a specific kind of happiness.
And that's when it really sucks, you know?
When it's specific.
When you can't feel the feeling
You so desperately need
And want to feel.
And it's so specific.
You start thinking of scenarios which will
Give that happiness to you
Without a doubt.
But what if that happiness
Means finding peace
In the freedom
Of letting go.
Of forgiving life
For not letting you feel-
Something you can so clearly see,
But can't ever touch.
Something left out in the open
In the Museum of Life;
Two inches away from touching it,
But then you see the sign.
    - *"Please Do Not Touch"*

140)

I used to be scared
Of being confrontational
Because
I was scared
Of losing relationships.
What if they got mad?
Or hurt?
Or upset?
But now, I'm more scared of losing myself.
What about my feelings?
My struggles?
My pain?

141)

I have a sort of violence inside of me
That's making me want to shout-
It's the type of monster
That you're scared to let out.
You're not sure just exactly what it looks like
Because you haven't seen it before.
But people keep feeding him
And you want him out your door.
They throw all kinds of things
Into your monster's cage.
You want to hyperventilate-
Pull your hair out-
Go insane.
I have this little monster-
This sort of violence in me.
And if I don't let it out,
It'll start eating away at my ability to be.

142)

Some people
Want to die.
While others
Fight for their life.

143)

Some days I feel like
Life's walking right through me.
As if it's just
Cleaning me out-
Watching me breathe.
I feel like a passenger in my own body.
Mold me-
Mold me like I'm putty.

144)

I remember
Wanting to get sick
So that I eat less,
Have an excuse to eat less-
And lose weight.
Only now do I know
That was a sickness too.

145)

Words
And
Bodies
Have
Trends
Just like clothes and accessories.
Forgive me if I'm not
Woke enough
To use the most lit language
In order to express that
Milkshakes have taken
A backseat to cake.

146)

Ladies going to
Blowout bars,
Sipping on cocktails
At 8 AM.
No need for money to be spent-
I get a free blowout each morning
By the subway vent.
    - *Thrifty & Swifty*

147)

So what if I want my daughter
To have a PhD
And she just
Wants to be a princess?
What if I teach her to be assertive
And she's passive?
What if my daughter is the opposite of me?
Well then,
I've taught her well.

148)

The more obsessed we are
With production-
With reproduction;
Weddings, babies, and tradition,
The more oppressed we become.
The more obsessed, the more oppressed.

149)

Don't confuse
Painful cramps
As punishment
For not getting
Pregnant.
We are not being
Punished for not
Being obedient.

150)

Vacation spots
Are hunted out
Through smells of
Tropical sunscreen
On the streets.

151)

When a woman gets grouped under a masculine label,
She embraces it.
When a man gets grounded under a feminine label,
He never forgives you for it.
Did you think I wrote
Groped
Instead of
Grouped?

152)

When people are afraid of risks,
I question their view on life.
Fearing risk
Assumes a position of ignorance that
The fear of truly living
Will put your ability
To fully live
At risk.
Sure, there's a risk of dying.
But then again,
There's always a risk of that.

153)

Our love
Was a passionate fireball
That forced through the space between us,
The space that encompassed all of our feelings.
Feelings of fear, of pain, of struggle, of vulnerability.
It burned through us,
Keeping our fire alive
And my mind often went to that place
When he wasn't around.
The more time we spent together,
The further our love burned.
And for once, I felt
The universe connected me
To itself.
We were both just bits of the universe
Dancing in space,
Colliding together,
Over and over,
Pushing our energy back and forth;
Magnetically finding our way back to our place
Of rejuvenation and elegance.

154)

Being a girl
Means being chained
To your phone.
Everyone fears for you,
So, you start to cling on to that
Until fear
Becomes comforting.

155)

Women are in competition
With each other.
Or, so it seems.
Who is the most oppressed?
They oppress themselves
And see who can do it best.
But is that best really worse
For society?
    - empower each other

156)
Will it last?
Whatever this is.
A blurring of lines;
Cravings of desires.
Desires of cravings.
Will this be
Anything close to
What we were hoping
It would be?
Clear up
This muddled water,
Signify my soul.
Desire is nothing
But a vast empty hole.

157)

For far too long I've felt,
The friendship of power
Slipping my hand.
I've tried to grasp it
Far too many times;
Each time more difficult;
Each time, a different disguise.

158)

They want me to dress all conservative
At work.
I feel sexless
Yet objectified.

159)
I try.
I try and I try
To assert myself
But every time
I have asserted myself in the past,
I have been
Punished
Or
Abandoned.
So, I cry.
I cry and I cry
Because I can't assert myself.
But every time
I don't assert myself,
I get praised and
Taken advantage of.
So, I
Yell at my therapist for being late,
I tell my boss my co-worker's hours aren't the same,
I tell my parents I can't handle their pain,
I tell myself there is more to be gained.

160)

Fear has silenced me for a while now.
It has paralyzed me.
Scared of speaking out.
Out of fear.
Are you really free
When you're chained down with fear?
Words are power,
And even more powerful when written down.
When ink hits the wood,
When millions of copies are printed...
There's something so real about the physical.
Something so official.
The pen can cut through more fear
Than any sword can.
And the taste of freedom
Will feel more near.

161)

Don't be clingy-
No, no.
Don't become enmeshed again.
Don't cling on to him-
No, no.
It's a self-fulfilling prophecy
And he'll leave you.
You feel insecure
So you
Punish yourself with
Imaginative thoughts
Of him cheating on you
With a hoe or a thot.
An Instagram model
Appears in your mind.
Tell him you love him and
Leave those distortions behind.

162)

When mourning
Turns to melancholia,
Morning
Turns to night.
Your closure is not yet attained,
So, you feel the dimming of the light.
Your gray becomes black
And your hope disappears.
You go from feeling
Anger and pain
To feeling like you'll never feel anything again.
You sleep so long
That you wake up in a coma.
You live but you don't really feel
The aroma.
Your flesh is cold
To the slightest touch
And your eyes ache
For that heavenly rush.
You want to be
Anywhere but here.
Caught between realms,
Life is no longer so dear.

163)

My anxiety
Is my baby-
I've given birth to it.
I feed it.
It's alive within me
And I feel it kicking in my tummy.
I feel it within me
And in attempt to avoid
Postpartum depression,
I never let it leave my body.

164)

The therapy room
Is a womb.
Small and comforting.
All encompassing.
A safe space
To be felt and heard.
You get nourished there
And nurtured.
The noise machine
Sounds like a sonogram.
Or what a baby would hear
When inside.
You grow in there
And then cry when you leave
Because you gotta say goodbye
And face the real world.
The cold, harsh reality of life.
But,
You take what you learned with you
And flourish.
What happened in the womb
Doesn't stay in the womb.
It goes with you
Wherever you do-
Impacting you for the rest of your life.
What the mind forgets,
The body remembers.

165)

I used to love knowing people's birthdays
And counting back nine months
To see what inspired their parents
Back then to have a baby.
I still love celebrating other people's birthdays,
But never my own.
Always looking for a way
To make somebody feel less alone.

166)

Her mom used to say that their sweet
old neighbor reminded her
Of her father
So, she couldn't tell her how he randomly hugged her one day
And said that she felt so good.
She couldn't tell her about the random
booty slap from a stranger
As she was exiting the subway at 4 pm one day
On her way back home to her mom.
When she yelled at him, the man claimed he was deaf
And then, another man walking down the same stairs
Mocked her for yelling at him.
She also couldn't tell her about a random man
Who whipped it out on the subway
And she had to change train cars.
When she did, police walked in with her
On that same new cart, but she froze
And didn't say a peep.
She does remember telling her
About the old man who groped her twice from behind
At their neighborhood CVS.
She froze back then too,
But she told her mom,
Who told her to scream louder next time.
She does now, but she gets mocked for it by other men.
She remembers the skirt she wore to the CVS that day.
She never wore it again.
It just sat there in her closet,

Elena Petrovska

Reminding her of the day she didn't scream loud enough.
She actually really liked that denim skirt
with purple fabric on the back.
But every time she thought about wearing it,
She had to think about how she'd fight back.

167)

There's not enough creativity in academia.
Mostly, it's run by men.
But even the women want to study just the hard
Math and sciences.
The phallic subjects.
Few appreciate creativity in academia
Now.
Which is a tragedy
Because creativity is art
And if we're getting a Bachelor of Arts
Or a Master of Arts,
Then where is the art?
Are we losing the passion and individuality
Of academia?
Even Freud went from the sciences to the arts;
From neurology to psychoanalysis.
But nobody likes Freud anymore.
So I feel alone.
I become a hysteric.
I act out,
I act out
I act out!
There's so much politics in academia
And people feel so scared of losing their PhD seat
That they don't stand up to the chairs.
But chairs and seats can move around
Like musical chairs.
And when the music stops,

Elena Petrovska

And the men stop dancing,
And I'm done standing up
(For myself),
I'll take a seat
At the big adult's table,
At the PhD table,
Right next to the co-chairs.

168)

Everyone is selfish.
Even when you give.
When you give some money
To the homeless lady,
You pay to feel better.
You pay for the relief
That your one or two dollars
Will spare her some grief.
You pay for your ego
To be boosted up a bit.
And you pay for yourself
To stop feeling like shit.

169)

Have you ever seen
A girl squirm with pleasure
When she says she feels
Powerful?
The feeling is orgasmic-
That feeling of power.
Have you ever seen her
Giggle with delight
When she speaks about being
Powerful?
Or were you too afraid
To even imagine the sight?

170)

Poems are like novels, you see.
Small tiny bits of stories
Pouring out of me.
All my life experiences
And stories I've heard-
Enough to make people feel something,
Even if it's absurd.
I had always wondered what it would
feel like to publish a book.
To feel it in my hands.
So one day,
I just started writing down all my ideas
During my most emotional and vulnerable
Time of the month.
Luckily for me,
It happened
Once a month.
And I turned the thing that I dreaded to get
To the thing that I couldn't wait to get.
Sure, it still hurt,
And yes, I was still bleeding.
But I never felt more alive
Than when the keyboard keys
Were hitting.

171)

I hate running.
On the treadmill, I mean.
No wonder it was a form of punishment-
So extreme.
And I wasn't motivated enough on my own,
So I joined a few classes
And I found that it felt like home.
Someone was screaming at me
To be better.
The more they yelled,
The more my forehead got wetter.
The girls around me-
They were my competition,
And toward the end,
I was starving from malnutrition.
But I lived for that hype-
I loved getting lost in the group.
I was such a good girl-
So obedient and aloof.
No room for my own thoughts,
I just had to comply.
No room for individualism-
If I didn't keep up-
Forget it, I'd rather die.

172)

You know when you look
Down at the toilet
And among the red water,
You see a few juicy, fat
Blood clots?
That's how I think of my poems.
Juicy, fat blood clots,
A collaboration of ideas
Swimming around
Some more diluted theories.

173)

So many rules about eating.
No breakfast or lunch- only dinner.
One meal a day and you'll be thinner.
Run on those eery apartment stairs,
Dance your belly away, and
Run with heavy layers.
Then, it was no sugar or sweets.
Only raw food for 3 weeks.
The scale dictated how much I'd eat that day,
So when I grew up,
Someone I loved threw the two I had away.
Since then, I've been scared to step on a scale.
I'm scared I'll freak out
And go back to that terrible time.
I now have no more rules
About what I eat.
I eat what I want
And I want what I eat.
I listen to my body
And in turn,
It actually listens to me.
When I want it to punch,
It punches, you see!
I want it to focus,
And that's just what it does.
I enjoy all my bites
And I prepare my food
With love.

174)

I feel pain.
I feel alive.
Pain is life.
My womb is shedding,
I bleed on my bedding.
I clean so much
On my period.
I've cleaned my own blood,
I've murdered myself.
I've taught myself to tolerate pain.
I've taught myself to inflict pain-
On nobody else but myself.

175)

Day 1, it's pretty light,
Something just emerges.
Day 2, it's more bright.
Day 3, it starts to get more heavy.
Day 4, it just pours right out of your belly.
That's how ideas flow
Right out of you.
They begin so small
And before you know it,
You've got even more to look forward to.

176)

Your mood
Dictates
Whether you wear a dress or pants,
Whether you listen to pop rock or acoustic sunrise,
Whether you go for a run or push your best downward dog,
Whether you wing your eyeliner or keep it straight,
Whether you put on a nude or vibrant pink nail polish,
Whether you make it on time to your therapy appointment or you're 20 minutes late,
Whether it's a chicken salad or pizza lunch kinda day,
And whether you wear heels or sneakers.

177)

Recovery is all about slowing things down.
Taking the extra time to
Display your food nicely,
Using only the finest plates and silverware.
Making it so pretty
So that you can eat with your eyes.
It's about realizing
That you need to
Feed yourself with the same beautiful love
That you give to everyone else
But yourself.

178)

Everyone who tries to leave me
Has to feel the pain I feel.
That is just how
I hold my own shield.
They abandon me
So I put my forces up
And prepare for violence.
I shield myself with the armor
Of silence.

179)

I'm a pusher,
I push people away.
The moment they become attached,
I no longer want them to stay.
Some call it cold-hearted,
Others call me a bitch.
I call it keeping my love contained and charted.
Quality over quantity
Is what I always desired.
And if the person takes too much of me,
They're fired.

180)

Why is being skinny so good?
What's so good about depriving yourself?
Why do you want me to make myself smaller?
To be less?
Does it say that I can say no to myself
Over and over?
But say yes to everyone else?
Does it say that I go against my body
And my needs and wants?
Does it say that I can conform?
Or that I can be who you want me to be?
What does it say
About you
To ask of me
To be something that I once wanted to be?
Something that caused me so much pain and shame?
What if I came to terms with myself
And you still want me to be skinny?
What then?
What's that say about you?

181)

Maybe if we stopped asking our children,
"What are you doing?"
"What are you wearing?"
"Who are you going with?"
"Why didn't you do this instead?"
"Where are you going?"
"When are you coming back home?"
And started asking them,
"How are you feeling?"
"Do you feel safe getting there?"
"How do your friends make you feel?"
"Do you feel safe coming back?"
"Is there anything I can do?"
We'd be able to teach them
To pay more attention to feelings
Than things that don't matter.
Are we asking the questions we're asking
For our children
Or for us?
Maybe if we stopped interrogating our children
And started caring- truly caring for them,
They would do the same
For everyone around them.

182)

Save my blood,
Save my pain,
Save my ashes-
Spread them in the rain.
Throw me in the river.
Toss me in wind.
Make them remember
How they all sinned.
Cut my love open,
Pull all strings attached;
I want them to know that
Our pain never matched.
They were thunder,
And I was a hurricane.
They loved the noise
And I carried the pain.

183)

A young teacher walked in to her first classroom.
Baby blue dress and blonde hair pinned neat,
She politely asked everyone to take their seat.
A little girl walked in to her first classroom.
Denim overalls and pigtails tied tight,
She repeated to herself that everything will be alright.
The teacher went around asking
What their parents do for them-
With all the best intentions to return
It all again.
The little girl listened
To all the toys bought-
The electronics and dolls,
Everything they ever sought.
When it was finally her turn,
She stood up and said-
My mama provides,
She provides for me-
A house full of hope and optimism, you see.
She feeds me stories
From books I want to read
And showers me
With love when I'm frustrated
And tug on her sleeve.
The other kids felt like they had everything they wanted-
But this.
This was a little harder to ask for
On a wish list.

184)

I know.
You find it easier
To discuss
Your scars;
But you keep
Your emotions
Behind barbed wires.

185)
She looked back at her burger,
Starved as she was,
Inhaling it in without any thought,
She recalled that familiar feeling
Of a loss of control while eating.
She realized
That maybe she didn't crave
All that ice cream and cookies and pizza
When she was younger.
But that she craved a feeling
Of a loss of control.
Because as nasty of a feeling as it was,
As nasty as the consequences of that feeling were,
That feeling provided her with a sense of comfort.
She had always felt passive.
Like she had no control
Of any situation around her.
That she wanted to act,
But her superego
Wouldn't listen.
So, she acted out.
In a way that broke all the rules,
Because they were stupid rules
To begin with.
So, she went back and forth
From the acceptable
To the forbidden.
Whether dictated by herself

ON MY PERIOD

Or others,
She was always searching for the middle ground,
But nobody presented that as an option.

186)

They give us free condoms
To protect us from pregnancy,
But they don't give us free pads and tampons
To deal with the aftermath of not having a baby.

187)

People think that
Just because I'm nice,
Kind-hearted,
Understanding,
And empathetic,
I am also naive.
That angers me.
I am not a flag
That's so easily swayed
By the wisp of the wind.
I am a wave
That feels whatever
Comes its way,
Hugs it,
And carries on.

188)
He's a good man.
He does the woman's work
Of pushing me.
To be better-
To stand on my own two feet;
Like a baby deer,
Whose mother nudges it to become independent.
He doesn't want me to be powerless.
He paces when he's powerless over my powerlessness.
Because he knows the feeling.
He's supportive.
And loyal.
And a man.
And mine.

189)

Dear Macedonia,
How does it feel
To have your name changed?
The price to fit in-
It's a hell of a deal.
My dear Macedonia,
So many ethnic wars.
Instead of opening windows,
We're closing doors.
Macedonia,
I'll hold you dear.
For you're a part of me,
And I'm a part of you.
But we all flourish, grow,
And evolve.
And with time,
More problems we'll solve.
My dear Macedonia,
You'll always be
Nothing less than
Macedonia to me.

190)

You know that feeling
When an image
Just sticks with you
So you have to write about it
And illustrate the life
That image brought to your mind?

191)

She was dancing on Capitalism's lap,
Making love to the bank
And the idea of the American dream.
She was nothing but a
Green beam;
Something to make
Gatsby proud.
"I love this hard cash!"
She moaned out loud.

192)

I remember reading a magazine article
One day
In a parenting magazine-
Because that's what I read when I was a teenager.
Because I would fantasize about being a mom.
I graduated from raising dolls
To reading Parents and Cosmo.
I came across an article
About how kids are less likely
To do drugs
If they eat dinner with their family
Every night.
Then, in college,
I read a journal article
About how kids are more likely
To develop eating disorders
If their families constantly argue
And debate
During dinner time.
So what good is not doing drugs
If you end up developing
An eating disorder?

193)

He walked in on the first day of class
And the room was dark,
But we were all sitting around, waiting,
Like obedient soldiers.
He walked in and glanced at us,
Turning the light on.
"Let there be light," he said.
And he enlightened us.

194)

She called me over for tea.
It was a nice spread of
Crackers, avocado, mozzarella cheese, almonds,
And the French truffles I brought.
I got lost on my way to her place.
I walked around her Brooklyn neighborhood
for about 45 minutes.
She understood, she said.
She didn't just say it- she meant it.
She felt it.
"Were you born here?" She asked.
"No- Macedonia." I answered.
She said that's why.
She moved around so much as a child.
And so did I.
We talked about getting used to that lost feeling.
We never got used to a place because our
environment was constantly changing.
My face lit up.
I wasn't getting lost because I was stupid,
Or bad at reading Google maps,
Or not even because I was a woman.
I was lost because I never got to know a place well enough.
No boundaries of what is mine and what is not.
The tea warmed my soul and I felt cherished.

195)

I stare at these words
That poured out of me
And gleam with pride.
I'm finally writing out
My honest feelings-
What a delight.

196)

When you're
Disobeying authority,
You could be obeying
The rules of mother nature,
And possibly, God.
That authority could be teaching you
To go against social justice
Because they just can't bear
You being a disgrace
With your choices.
Yet, the force of nature-
The push and pull of humanity
Could be whispering to you,
"Do it, do it, this is the right choice."
You could be the hero
Of your generation
And still get yelled at
By people.
Who are you disobeying
By obeying them?
Yourself?
Love?
Life?
And who are they disobeying
By saying they know what's best for you?

197)

My sisters
Are my keepers
Of pain and laughter.
They're my protectors
From pain and harm.
My sisters are my
Safe home
When all else fails
And the world sinks in.
They're my anchors,
Who reel me back
To where I've always been.

198)

Dancing with the newborn sand
On a beach in Montauk.
There she was by my hand,
Relieving me of shell shock.
The waves-
They scared me.
But she-
She didn't care.
There was something about her riskiness
That made my life feel unfair.
I looked at him,
I looked at her-
Both surfing through the waves of life.
Letting themselves be carried
By anything in their sight.
I looked at me.
I stepped back.
Facing waves
Gave me a heart attack.
I stopped at the very place
Where the waves break
And she looked back laughing, as I started to shake.
"That's the thing about anxiety-
You freeze at the very worse part."
I looked at my thighs,
The waves crashing in.
It was almost as if I was used to the pain.
I walked in further and dove right in,

ON MY PERIOD

Letting my body be carried
By the waves of life.
No longer here nor there-
No longer anxiety or despair.
She helped me go deeper-
Deeper, you see.
That's what a psychoanalyst did to me.

199)

What if
You reject people
Because you think you don't deserve them?
What if
You reject people
Because you are so scared of getting rejected
That you reject them
Before they ever get a chance to reject you?

200)

I remember my dad
Taking me to the movies
For one of my birthdays.
We share loose teas
And talk about the latest technology.
We have the same dad jokes and
That's where I got it from, I guess.
We talk and debate a lot.
They say I look like him
And I wonder if he still sometimes
Sees himself in me.

201)

A little boy
Sitting on the LIRR
Asked his mom
How he was related to his father.
To which his mother said,
"How are you related to daddy? Really?"
And the little boy said,
"But how? He didn't born me."
And then proceeded to sit on her lap,
As she gently pushed him off.

202)

They want you
To be a little bored
At work
So you can do some internet shopping
On your off time
And maintain capitalism.

203)

Watch the demographics change
On crowded New York trains.
They say it's all one big melting pot
But this hustle and bustle
Makes me think it's not.

204)

I hold my boobs
As I run
Because I was taught to
Hide my body from guys.

205)

Sometimes,
I re-read my own writing
And forget I even wrote that.
I repress my pain,
But my words remind me again.

206)

Baking is an art.
Each step of adding ingredients
Has beauty in it.
And if the kitchen is well lit
With natural lighting,
You're a modern day Da Vinci.
I don't feel oppressed when I bake;
I feel free.
Free to add whatever I like,
Taste the batter whenever I like,
And free to be creative.
There's care
And love
Baked into every
Delicacy.
And freedom- lots of freedom.
I got this love for fine confectionary
From my grandmothers and mother.
    - *Sublimation*

207)

When people keep commenting
On the weight of your body,
Whether heavier or thinner,
You learn that you amount to nothing more than your looks.
That's the weight of being embodied.
They think they're helping you-
They think they're complimenting you.
But nobody knows what goes on behind
Locked bathroom doors
With the faucet running.

208)

He told me I'm sensitive.
But they would say I'm in touch or
Something more elegant, like introspective.
But he's right- I am sensitive.
Sensitive is an egg shell, waiting to be cracked into life.
Sensitive is a rose that you should handle
with ease and enjoy from afar.
Sensitive is a cloud, which can pour down some snow.
Sensitive is me, waiting to explode.

209)

People weren't made for living together
Unless there's a romantic tie
Between them
And something worth fighting for.
The only way humans
Can live with other humans
Is if there is some sort of emotional connection-
Something worth repairing
When all hell breaks loose.
When the dishes aren't done,
When the sleeping schedules
And noise levels
Don't align,
At least the love is still intertwined.

210)

The wounds
From our womb
Become the womb
For our wounds.
We carry them as we grow.

211)

I see her-
Walking, walking-
BOOM.
Her eye catches his profile.
Quick feet, quick feet.
She puts down the milk
And the chocolate-
The chocolate she was craving since last week.
She rushes to leave-
Quick feet, quick feet,
Don't look, don't look.
If he sees her, she'll have to say hi
And hug
And pretend that it's ok
That he has a wife
And a kid at home
And is still trying to make moves on her.
OUT.
Back into the building next door.
Swipe- she's in.
She can relax-
No.
Never mind.
He's here.
She has to embrace it.
She cries inside.
She plays with her phone.
She pushes the elevator button.

ON MY PERIOD

She pretends she doesn't see him,
But he sees her.
"Hi!"
She makes up an excuse…"I'm in a rush," she says.
Always in some kind of rush
To avoid men.

212)

Periods are messy.
Womanhood is messier.
Cramps are painful.
Childbirth is more painful.
Cravings are annoying.
Waking up in the middle of the night is more annoying.

213)

Do your scars ever
Look back at you
When you're salting the dinner steak?
Or perhaps in the shower,
When the water beats on your face?
I imagine you feel the pain so clear,
That it burns you inside
When it's the screams that you hear.
A silent kind of violent cry,
Screaming for something more this time.
Impulsive, restless.
You're just cutting a void into your skin
That looks a lot like the space you're trying to fill.

214)

Our bosses
Toss us around
Like the overpriced salad
They bought for lunch.
They dress us up
In whatever flavor they'd like that day.
And if we're not right enough for them,
They'll dispose us.
Because there's always another salad
That will accept the pleasure of being
Chewed up and eaten out
By someone in a position of power.

215)

They say all is fair in love and war.
Show me the way to the one I adore.
I love you, I hate you.
I love you to pieces.

216)

We can say we don't need it,
But deep, deep down,
There's a painful longing
For our parent's approval.

217)

The more you try to contain me,
Tie me down,
Chain me,
The more I have a craving for art.
I need that outlet;
That emotional pitfall.
Take everything away,
And I'll still have my words,
And I'll still have my blood.

218)

There was more to those eyes than just the things they saw.
Eyes are funny.
Sometimes, when you ask someone
To remove their glasses,
It's so you can have the privilege of
Seeing them more clearly
At the expense of their 20/20 eyesight.
And sometimes, when you look close enough
In someone's eyes,
You not only see the person,
But you also see yourself
In them.

219)

Some women sometimes wear
A wedding ring
So that men don't bother them.
And if you think this stops them,
You and I should talk again.

220)

Maybe she'll keep chasing
All that external validation
Forever
Because she'll never get it
From the very place she first sought it-
Her creators.

221)

Poetry is a confession
Of secrets
Held in for so long.
A sealed mouth
Screaming to be let loose.
A curse of the soul-
A disciplined quietness-
It can make you feel
So much
With so many limitations.
Come witness the confines of my heart
And the desperation of my body.

222)

Love
That can transcend
Time,
Space,
Race,
Gender,
Religion,
Culture,
And ethnicity
Is a love
That's truly
Worth keeping.
That kind of love
Does not take itself for granted,
And doesn't value materiality.
That kind of love
Doesn't place
More importance on social constructions
Than the individuals, themselves.

223)

If blood is emotion,
I've been writing in
Nothing but blood.
I've been pouring my
Blood out on paper
And my sins on the rug.
I've been saving it
For you to read
Instead of disposing of it
For nobody to see.
Do
You
See
Me?

224)

I remember the anarchist
Telling us the story of her daughter
Picking out shoes.
The shoes were glittery and sparkly
And didn't look the greatest on her,
But she still liked them.
She liked the way they looked from the top, looking down.
And maybe that's a metaphor for life.
Others may not always like our walk of life
Because they're looking at it from a
different perspective than we are.
They may not like our walk of life because it's too
Shiny,
Or glittery,
Or sparkly,
Or dull.
But, it may be the most comfortable and
beautiful from our perspective.

225)

The doctor told me
I had secretive ovaries.
They were hiding
And we couldn't find them on the sonogram.
The next day,
I told my analyst
It was all psychosomatic.
    - Hysteric

226)

Timing-
Just like in life,
Is everything in poetry.

227)

I remember someone once told me
That a poem is never finished-
It is only abandoned.
Perhaps it's because
The poet is constantly
A growing and evolving individual.
Don't abandon your growth.

228)

Hunt for all the things
That make me up
And I'll gather the analyses
That take up
My unconscious waters
Rising up.
Hunt for everything
I've lost in myself.
The forests of my trees of thoughts;
Dig up the roots and bring them to me,
But handle them so delicately.
I'll continue building up crooked walls
So you can tear them down
Because they weren't even that sturdy
Before you came around.
Hunt for the self that I've lost.
Hunt for the desires under my thoughts.
Hunt all these things
And I'll gather them up.
To rebuild myself with actual love.
Carry your shotgun
To rupture holes in my irrationality
And shoot all your ammunition at
The animals in me.
These animals-
They've lived in me for too long,
But now they've started to devour my life's song.

229)

Dancing, prancing,
He makes my heart sing.
Dancing is flirting
With life.
He guides us through
All the motions.
Dancing is communication, he says.
I take his lead on this advance.
1-2-3-4
Side to side,
1-2-3-4
I won't hide.
1-2-3-4
Until sweat pours out,
1-2-3-4
My body begins to shout.
A smile emerges on my face,
He teaches us with such elegant grace.
This moment
Extends to everyday life,
Dancing is therapeutic
To a marriage in fright.
There is beauty in the dance,
Beauty in the ways
We miscommunicate
Just to find ourselves in a daze.
Somehow life finds us,
And brings us to our knees.
Somehow we find each other
When there is a serendipitous breeze.

230)

Instead of self-medicating
With booze and drugs,
Why not
Up the dose of your therapy sessions
Instead?

231)

They say laughter is the best medicine.
Cherry or grape,
Dark humor or stand up,
Everyone's got a different taste
In both.
We can only know medicine
If we know pain.
We can only know laughter
If we suffer again.

232)

The lack
Is not in the other.
It's in yourself.
The lack
Is not in yourself.
It's in the other.
Who lacks who?

233)

They say there's life in me,
But I hold death in my hand.
I've got the ability to
Swing a punch at myself
All over and over, over again.

234)

The mind may slip away
From the truth,
But the body-
The body remembers.
    - *Unconscious*

235)

Harrassment
Because some people only want to talk about what
Her ass meant / Harrassment
And not what she meant.

236)

For some,
Therapy is a threat
"Don't get better."
"Don't change."
"You'll get in trouble if you do."

237)

First taste of a drug,
Like love-
Heavenly, divine, pleasure above.
Rest of the relationship to a drug,
Grieving for that first kiss.
Nothing will ever be enough,
Addiction is like grieving
For a love you'll never get back.
Recovery is healing,
Allowing yourself to feel again.

238)

Past trauma is like
A video game.
Let me pass the level
Or play it again.
Over and over,
Until it's resolved.
A different level,
The same song.

239)

Sometimes I talk back,
Sometimes I talk back
When I get cat called
Because if I don't,
I feel even more like an object.
   - *Ovary-acting*

240)

End this punishment.
I've been in this corner for far too long.
Put an end to this sentence.
This sentence has become a broken song.
She says my period
Has lasted for years.
I've committed no crime,
Yet I'm wearing nothing but tears.
Glazed face and cakey cover-up,
To put on a mask for all to see.
I'm a woman with a need
For the reality of fantasy.
A confusion rises up in my blood-
Take these broken legs
Out from the sinking mud.
What kind of cruel mind
One must have,
To sentence their life
As if it is death.
Fix these broken legs
And walk on your own.
Fix your jail of a mind
And call it a home.
This period
Has lasted for far too long,
This period has prolonged every wrong.
This period should end,

ON MY PERIOD

Just as this poem
And book should too.
And even this sentence will end with pure virtue.
 - *Period*

About the Author

Elena Petrovska was born in Macedonia and raised in New York. She is currently attending The New School for Social Research's Psychology graduate program in New York City. Apart from reading and writing, Elena enjoys spending time in nature, especially with her loved ones.

www.ingramcontent.com/pod-product-compliance
Lightning Source LLC
Chambersburg PA
CBHW030107100526
44591CB00009B/316